Comfort & Hope

Uplifting Poetry

by

Christine V Mitchell

Copyright © 2014 Christine V Mitchell

COMFORT & HOPE
by Christine V Mitchell

First published 2014

All rights reserved solely by the author. No part of this publication may be reproduced, stored in a retrieval system or transmitted in any form or by any means - electronic, mechanical, photocopied, recorded or otherwise - except for brief quotation in printed reviews, without the prior written consent of the author.

Interior images (originally) by
kozzi.com; morguefile.com

Scripture quotations taken from the Holy Bible
King James Version (KJV)
(unless otherwise stated)

Written, compiled and prepared for publishing by the author
Copyright registered with Copyright House

All poetry
registered
with
Copyright House

ISBN-10: 1500139696
ISBN-13: 978-1500139698

CONTENTS

Acknowledgements v
Introduction 1

1. COMFORT OF HIS LOVE

Come Walk With Me 4
Brand New Start 6
My Peace 7
Living Water 9
There's A Love 10
I Was There 11
Your Shepherd 12
Just A Moment 13
Look Up 14
Hope Always 16
No Greater One 17
Reach for Gold 18

2. CHALLENGES & TEMPTATION

At This Gate 22
You Made It This Far 24
He Has Time for You 25
Never Forgotten 27
Pray 28
Just When You Thought It Was Over 29
He'll Be There 31
He Never Leaves 32

3. PRAYERS

To You I Cling 36
I'm Turning It Over! 37
Shine Me A Light 38
Deep In My Heart 39
A Prayer for Healing 40
Quiet Moments 41
Bless Families 42
Each Day 43
Where Shall I Go? 44
I Just Need to Know 45

4. COMFORT IN SORROW

Now That You've Gone 48
It Will Be Worth It All 49
He Cares for You 50
Just A Dream 52
Blessed Are They That Mourn 53
A Day Is Coming 55
Beyond the Sunset 56

SPECIAL PRAYER

Come Into My Heart 58

About the Author 61

ACKNOWLEDGEMENTS

I am truly thankful to God for His gift of love, my wonderful Saviour, the Lord Jesus Christ, and for the privilege and honour of being able to share His love with you through poetry. I give Him all praise and glory. Without Him, none of this would have been possible.

I wish to thank my wonderful family so much - my husband Frederick and our children (young adults) - for their patience, support and encouragement during the preparation of this work, and for their help in the final proof-reading and editing.

Special 'thank you' to my dear cousin-in-law, author and poet Rev Lydia Woodson-Sloley (USA), for her wonderful and encouraging words always. Thanks also to a dear friend, poet and author Sandra Stoner-Mitchell and other friends, poets and writers for their encouragement, advice and support.

"They that trust in the Lord
shall be as Mount Zion,
which cannot be removed,
but abides forever"
(Psalm 125:1)
KJV 2000

INTRODUCTION

Comfort & Hope is an inspirational collection of heartfelt poems filled with words of encouragement and consolation that will help during difficult seasons in life, such as grief, distress, loneliness, despair and uncertainty.

When faced with challenges, coping can be difficult. Others may depend on us to be at our best while, deep within, we may be crying out for help. The pain of sorrow may seem insurmountable and life's trials may cloud our vision. It may even be hard to pray and we may feel that God is far away. Sharing our burdens may be difficult, as others may not understand or we may find their words offer little or no comfort. There is hope today, dear friend.

Within these pages, you will find words of love and reassurance that will uplift your soul and shine light upon your path. Heartfelt prayer poems are included which may echo the cry of your heart. The poems can be read at any time of the day and anywhere. Some are written as poetic 'letters' or expressions from the Lord to you, such as "Come Walk With Me" and "I Was There". Many are accompanied by Biblical references.

Throughout my life, I have faced many difficult challenges. I know for certain that without the all-embracing comfort and love of the Lord that sustained and strengthened me during those seasons, I would not be where I am today. It's awesome to know that, despite my shortcomings, His unconditional love reaches out again and again - lifting me up and giving me hope as I look up to Him. He is the Author and Finisher of my faith (Hebrews 12:2).

Strangely, many of my experiences were stored deep in my heart for a very long time until one day, some years ago, when God began to inspire me to write poetry. As I began writing poem after poem, most of which is centred on my faith, I found myself blessed and wanted to share these blessings with others also. This is what led me to produce my first book of poetry, Forever Grateful (published January 2014).

My greatest joy has been receiving messages of how my poems have deeply touched and held special meaning to readers. The Lord is my inspiration and deserves all the glory. My journey with Him continues to be one of discovering more about the preciousness of His love.

My purpose in producing this book is to help shine the light of His love through poetic words of comfort that I pray will bring hope and reassurance in troubled times. The Lord can take the broken pieces of our lives and put them back together.

Whatever your situation or season, I encourage you to explore this collection and pray that you will be inspired on your life's journey, and realise how very much God loves and cares for you. Thank you so much for reading! God bless you!

Christine V Mitchell

Chapter 1

Comfort of His Love

ঌ

*Jesus said:
"...and, lo, I am with you alway, even
unto the end of the world. Amen"
(Matthew 28:20).*

~~ COME WALK WITH ME ~~

Come take a walk with Me
and leave behind the cares of yesterday.

Come take some time aside,
for I'll be there to hear you when you pray.

So many are the years
I know you've longed for change to come your way.

I've seen your many tears;
you felt deep down that I was far away.

If only you could see
how many times I tried to be your Friend.

If only you could know
how much I longed your broken heart to mend.

There is a secret place
within your heart where heaven's light will shine;

A place where you can know
My lasting peace to calm your troubled mind.

If you'll open the door,
I will come in and never leave your side.

I'll be your Everything.
I'll be your Help, your Comfort and your Guide.

Come take a walk with Me.
Give Me your heavy burdens and your load.

My heart is meek and lowly;
in Me you will find rest along life's road.

Come take a walk with Me.
It's My desire to cheer your heart today.

My heart is full of love.
I'm close to you, I'm listening as you pray.
--o0o--

(Matthew 11:28)

~~ A BRAND NEW START ~~

How do you bring back stolen years,
blown away in the wind?
How do you fan a dwindling flame
on which your hopes were pinned?

How can you have a brand new start
when others won't forget
the past you long to leave behind,
that causes you to fret?

Jesus offers hope today
for a bright and new tomorrow.
The sins of the world were laid on Him,
He bore our grief and sorrow.

In Him you can have a brand new start.
He'll cause new life to spring
for He is the Way to eternal life,
a life that begins within.
--oOo--

(Isaiah 53:3; John 1:29; John 14:6; 2 Corinthians 5:17)

~~ MY PEACE ~~

My peace I leave with you.
Though I have gone away,
the Comforter has come;
He'll teach you how to pray.

My peace I leave with you.
I know the cross you bear.
I've walked the road before you.
I know, for I've been there.

My peace I leave with you.
Though some may turn away,
My presence will be with you
throughout each night and day.

My peace I leave with you.
Amidst all tribulation,
you'll know My peace within
and lasting consolation.

My peace I leave with you.
Amidst the toil and strife,
just focus on My words
for they are words of life.

My peace I leave with you;
calm waters and serene.
The fountain of My peace
will be a living stream.

Let not your heart be troubled.
Don't let it be afraid,
for the peace I leave with you
no-one can take away.
--oOo--

(John 14:16 and 27)

~~ LIVING WATER ~~

Thirsty soul, need a drink?
Parched inside? On the brink?
Is your well now running dry?
Is your need not satisfied?

Come to Me, Christ the Giver
of living water, like a river.
There's no cost; needs no money.
It is sweeter than all honey.

Deep within, it shall flow;
quench your thirst, give a glow!
In your heart, refreshing rain!
You will never thirst again!

Lasting joy from heaven above
you will have, with peace and love!
Thirsty soul, receive from Me
water of life eternally!
--oOo--

(John 4; John 7:37)

~~ THERE'S A LOVE ~~

There's a love that's like no other.
It's a love that's from on high.
There's none like it in this world,
the love of God for you and I.
Breaking barriers, building bridges,
reaching high and low alike,
it can overcome the darkness
with its penetrating light.

It's a love that brings forgiveness
and will pardon every sin.
It is found in Christ the Saviour,
as we ask Him to come in.
It's a love that says "You're special".
It's a love that calls you "Friend".
If you open up your heart, you'll find
it's a love that never ends.

--oOo--

(Ephesians 3:19)

~~ I WAS THERE ~~

I was there when you went through the darkness.
I was there when you couldn't see light;
when your troubles were just like a shroud,
as they hid all My blessings from sight.
`I was there when the world turned its back.
I was there when your skies were so grey;
when a friend was nowhere to be found
or you felt that you'd gone far astray.

As the dewdrops descend in the morning,
as the stars up above fill the sky,
as the sunshine in Summer or Winter,
in all seasons, My presence is nigh.
As you walk through this life on your journey,
never knowing what you'll face each day,
just remember that I'm always with you.
I am only a prayer away.
--o0o--

(Psalm 139:1-17; Matthew 28:20b)

~~ YOUR SHEPHERD ~~

How great and precious is the Lord,
the Shepherd of your soul;
you'll find you're never wanting -
when He is in control.

In pastures green, near silent streams,
your soul He will restore.
In righteous paths, the Lord will lead;
He walked the road before.

Even in the darkest valley,
you will know He's near.
His presence will surround you and
you'll have no need to fear.

When gloomy shadows seem to fall
or dark clouds gather round,
His words of life will comfort you
and lasting peace abound.

In the presence of your enemies,
He'll feed your hungry soul,
anointing you with oil divine;
your cup will overflow.

The goodness and the mercy of
the Lord will follow you.
Each day until forever, He's
the One Who'll see you through.
--oOo--

(Job 23:10; Psalm 23)

~~ JUST A MOMENT ~~

All that He asks is a moment of time.
In quiet surrender, His peace is sublime.
The world crashes in through its noise and demands
in things that we see
and the thoughts of our minds.
As wave upon wave crashes on the seashore,
the world crashes in and keeps asking for more.
Just a moment aside, to gaze on His face;
a moment with Jesus, the Giver of grace.
He patiently waits with rivers of peace,
of comfort and joy He longs to release
in hearts that will give Him a moment of time
to bask in His presence, a moment divine.
--oOo--

(Psalm 16:11b)

~~ LOOK UP ~~

If birds should stop their singing
or sparrows fail to fly;
if oceans, lakes and rivers
should suddenly be dry.

If mellow moonlight hides away
or stars refuse to shine,
one thing will stand forever,
God's precious love divine.

If suddenly the flavour
of life has disappeared;
if raging storms and fiery trials
have left you feeling seared.

If when you've done your best, you feel
it's never good enough,
The Lord will be your comfort -
in the smooth and in the rough.

Look up beyond the clouds;
there's more than meets the eye,
for way above the floating fluff
a brilliance fills the sky.

Look up in faith to heaven
to Him Who dwells on high;
on all who reverence Him,
the Son of Righteousness will rise.

Though things of earth on which you lean
at times may seem to fail,
His all-embracing love unseen,
to you He will unveil.

Look up to God, for He is light
and again your heart will sing.
In Him you'll find the breath of life
that changes everything!
--o0o--

(Psalm 121:1-2)

~~ HOPE ALWAYS ~~

Hope, when doubts assail you.
Hope, when around you looks grim.
<u>Your God will never fail you;</u>
<u>just anchor your hope in Him.</u>

Hope, when the mountains are crumbling.
Hope, when you feel insecure.
His steadfast love never ceases;
it's a love that will always endure.

Hope, when there's nowhere to turn.
<u>Hope, when you need peace of mind.</u>
<u>Trust in the words of the Saviour;</u>
His words are healing and kind.

Each day has a brand new dawning;
ever faithful the skies above.
Each day and new every morning,
we can hope in the Saviour's love.

--oOo--

~~ NO GREATER ONE ~~

I walked in the garden of peace one day,
as I knelt before the throne
of Christ my Saviour, King and Friend;
I came to Him alone.
I could not speak for tears that flowed
gave voice to my heart's sorrow.
I knew that He would not condemn;
He gives me hope for tomorrow.
No greater one on earth could meet me
at my point of need.
I bore my soul to Him Whose love
is the love that sets me free.
The grace He poured into my soul
is the grace that helps me live;
it's the grace that heals me deep within
and helps me to forgive.
Through Him I can arise once more
and journey on my way.
Dear friend, the love of Jesus can also
heal your soul today.

--o0o--

~~ REACH FOR GOLD ~~
(A-Z)

Allow yourself to rest tonight.
Bask in the peace of Christ, your Light.
Clear your mind of doubts and fears.
Don't let worry steal the years.

Emancipate the hope within.
Faith will help you fight and win -
Giving you the grace to stand;
Helping you reach the "promised land".

It may not be very long.
Just hold on now, just be strong.
Keep on smiling in the race.
Love will come with warm embrace.

Motivated by your dreams,
Never give up though it seems
Others may be moving on.
Press ahead and sing your song.

Quietly, the sun will rise.
Rays of hope will fill the skies.
Strength anew will come to you,
Touching everything you do.

Underneath you may have cried,
Void of hope though you have tried.
With God's help along life's map,
X-ray all the thoughts that sap.

You can reach new heights untold.
Zero in and reach for gold!
--o0o--

(Revelation 3:11)

Chapter 2

Challenges & Temptation

❦

Jesus said:
".. I will pray the Father,
and He shall give you another Comforter,
that He may abide with you forever"
(John 14:16)

~~ AT THIS GATE ~~

When will my change come?
Has the time passed?
Is it now too late?
So long .. sitting here
alone at this gate.

Everyone rushes on.
They dip ... they dip into the blessing;
they run along, singing their song.
But here I wait .. at this gate.
I toss and I turn;
deep within .. I burn with desire
to live on a higher plain.

"Please .. don't walk away".

My cry, just another sound,
like the rustle of leaves
swayed in a gentle breeze.
No startling storm.. just the norm.
I am to them as a pebble misplaced.

A shadow passes near,
the shadow of a heavenly light.
Suddenly, all fear dissolves
as the voice of Love
says to me
"Arise ... take up your mat
and walk".

Each day, each hour,
like a flower parched of rain,
I felt withered.
I dithered and paused;
felt I had a cause.

But now, now I arise..
I arise! I'm ALIVE!
I leave that space.
I join life's race.
I see myself through His eyes,
the eyes of Love.
He makes me complete.
New strength grips my heart,
my soul, my feet!

No longer will I wait
at this gate.
--o0o--

(John 5:2-9)

~~ YOU MADE IT THIS FAR ~~

You made it this far
though the road was rough,
though trials you faced
seemed more than enough.

Though some days were lonely
and all looked bleak,
you trusted the Saviour
to guide your feet.

At times when it seemed
you could go on no longer,
His word came through and
helped you to be stronger.

He was beside you,
the Star in your night;
so true and so faithful,
Whose burden is light.

He promised to be with you,
right to the end.
Keep trusting in Jesus,
Your Saviour and Friend!
--o0o--

(Hebrews 10:35; Psalm 125:1)

~~ HE HAS TIME FOR YOU ~~

He has time for you,
whatever time you pray.
He has time for you,
at any time of day.

When words cannot express
the longings deep within,
your heart, in quietness,
can still reach out to Him.

He has time for you,
when some don't understand.
He has time for you,
when things don't look so grand.

The burden may be great,
or even if it's small,
His ear is always listening
to hear you when you call.

He has time for you.
He'll cleanse you from all sin.
He has time for you.
He'll free you from within.

Whatever you may need,
He's right there by your side;
and if you call His Name,
He hears your faintest cry.

He has time for you.
His presence is so real.
He has time for you.
He comforts and He heals.

The path ahead you'll run
with strength to win the race
and help from God above,
Who gives enabling grace.

He has time for you.
Will you make time for Him?
He's Christ, the Lord and greatest Friend
of all who let Him in.
--oOo--

(John 6:37)

~~ NEVER FORGOTTEN ~~

Never forgotten are the hands of love
that toil behind the scenes;
the feet that tread the lonely path
where few have ever been;
the heart in which compassion's river
readily can flow;
the ears that listen patiently
as a burdened soul unloads;
the nights of toil when, in the darkest
hour, prayers are prayed;
the sacrifice of love that lifts
a soul that is dismayed.
the mind that thinks upon good things
of purity, life and peace;
the person in whose heart the love
of God can find release.
The Lord is not unrighteous to
forget your labour of love.
Keep doing your best, for great is your
reward in heaven above.
--oOo--

(Matthew 5:7-8; Philippians 4:8; Hebrews 6:10)

~~ PRAY ~~

When hope is gone and your heart's song
has flown away - pray.
When it's hard to rise and darkened skies
exist above you - pray.

In a stormy gale, when people fail
and you're all alone - pray.
When burdens increase and you need relief
deep down inside - pray.

Just call on the Name of Jesus for He
hears you, as you pray.
He dwells on high, but He is nigh
to all who humbly pray.

He'll give you peace, the storms will cease
and fears decrease - just pray.
He's there for you. He's faithful and true;
in all that you do, as you pray.

Pure as a dove, His voice of Love
is calling you today.
Tenderly and patiently,
He's listening, as you pray.
--o0o--

(Luke 18:1; 1 Thessalonians 5:17)

~~ JUST WHEN YOU THOUGHT ~~
IT WAS OVER

Just as the clouds were clearing,
when at last the sun shone through,
when swirling seas looked calm,
serene and tranquil the view.

Just when you let down your guard,
just when you thought you could rest,
just when you thought it was over,
along came another test.

Tired of fighting more battles?
The King of glory has seen.
Alone, we can never make it;
we need His strength within.

Who is this King of glory?
The Lord Almighty is He;
mighty in battle to save us.
He sets the captives free.

Mountains will melt before Him.
At His word, the waves must cease.
Over heaven and earth He reigns -
Jesus, the Prince of Peace.

Your weeping may long have endured.
It may seem your night will not end,
but joy will come in the morning;
this IS God's promise, dear friend.

He's the Healer of broken hearts,
Christ Jesus, the King of kings;
always ready, His love to impart.
One touch can change everything.

Believe His unfailing promise
and trust His word today.
Don't fret! Look up! Hold on!
Your answer is on the way!
--oOo--

(Psalm 24:7-10; Psalm 30:5; Isaiah 55:10-11; Mark 4:35-40; Luke 4:18; 1 Timothy 6:14-15)

~~ HE'LL BE THERE ~~

Be strong and of good courage.
Don't let the sights dismay.
He'll be there in the battle.
He will not let you stray.

If the Lord our God is for us,
then who can be against?
For He's our Mighty Fortress;
our Shield and our Defence.

No weapon formed shall prosper;
no judging tongue succeed.
In Christ we are forgiven;
our righteousness is He.

Hold fast to His mighty word,
for greater is He in you
than he that is in the world.
The Lord will see you through.
--oOo--

(Joshua 1:9; Isaiah 54:17; Romans 8:31; 1 John 4:4)

~~ HE NEVER LEAVES ~~

Friends may be there in the sunshine,
God is still there when it rains.
Their love may be there for a time,
His love for you always remains.
Though others may hurry away,
the Lord waits patiently -
for He has the time of day
and He listens lovingly.

Just stand on His life-giving words
and never let feelings dictate,
for things you've not seen or heard
will begin as you hold on in faith.
Keep trusting in Him and believe
and you'll be amazed to see
He's the God Who never leaves;
that's how much He loves you and me.
--o0o--

(Isaiah 41:10; Matthew 28:20)

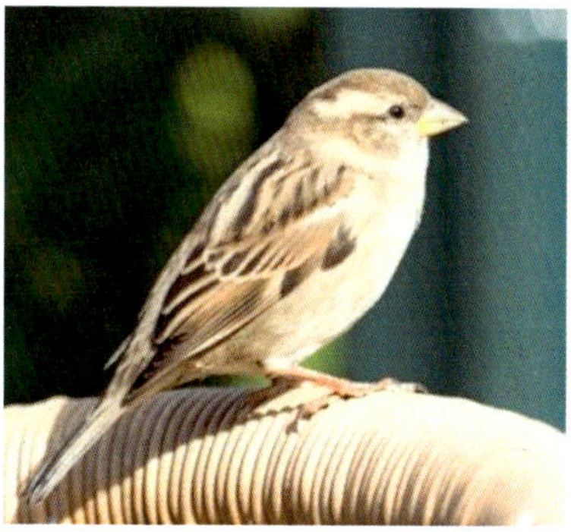

Chapter 3

Prayers

ೲ

*"Casting all your care upon Him;
for He careth for you"
(1 Peter 5:7)*

~~ TO YOU I CLING ~~

O Father, in Your tender mercy,
hold me up, for I am weak.
There's no-one that I desire
but You alone, it's You I seek.

I come in the precious Name of Jesus
Christ my Lord, my Saviour and King;
empty-handed, claiming nothing,
drawn by love, to You I cling.

Whisper words within my spirit.
Give me strength that I may stand,
not by my own human effort
but by the power of Your strong hand.

Lead me Saviour, Friend and Shepherd;
let me always hear Your voice.
In the hour of temptation,
help me to make a righteous choice.

Touch me, Lord, in Your tender mercy.
Draw me closer every day.
May Your heart's desire be
my highest joy, dear Lord, I pray.

--oOo--

(Psalm 73:25)

~~ I'M TURNING IT OVER! ~~

I'm turning it over to You Lord.
I've tried too hard this time.
My strength at best is feeble.
I'm in need of Your power divine.
I'm turning it over to You Lord.
O why did I stay so long
when patiently You were waiting
with grace to make me strong?

I'm turning it over to You Lord.
Please help me now to listen;
to see amidst the stars that shine,
Yours is the one that glistens.
O Lord, I now surrender.
Whatever Your will entails,
may I give up, in total trust –
knowing You never fail!
--oOo--

(2 Corinthians 12:9)

~~ SHINE ME A LIGHT ~~

Shine me a light in the darkness,
when the way I just cannot see.
Give me an anchor that holds,
when the waters are troubling me.

I need a light in the tunnel;
can't wait till I get to the end.
O Saviour, I need You right now,
for You are a faithful Friend.

I know that You hear when I call.
You never have turned me away.
O shine me a light in the darkness,
dear Lord, as I humbly pray.

When others don't understand,
when they say there are worse than me,
not knowing I need a strong hand,
not seeing the things I have seen;

Not knowing the depths of my pain,
the despair and the anguish within;
O Lord send Your comforting presence.
Please help me to stand again.

Let my prayer come before Your throne.
Lord arise with Your healing wings.
O shine me a light in the darkness,
that my soul once again may sing.
--oOo--

(Psalm 18:6)

~~ DEEP IN MY HEART ~~

Deep in my heart, I will rejoice.
Waiting in hope, I'll lift up my voice.
Why should I now let my soul be cast down?
I'll hope in my God, for He'll keep me sound.
For I will yet praise Him, beholding His face.
The help of His countenance gives me more grace.
Assured of His love, I'll continue to pray,
for He is my joy - my strength for each day.
Waiting in hope, the Lord is my choice,
so deep in my heart, I will rejoice.
--oOo--

(Psalm 42:5 and 11)

~~ A PRAYER FOR HEALING ~~

Lord, I'm waiting in Your presence.
Saviour, help me to be strong.
When my faith is tried, O help me;
when it seems I can't wait long.

For this trial is a mountain
and this darkness leaves me numb.
Lord, I need You, precious Jesus;
Oh I need You now to come.

Take away this heavy burden.
Lord, I place it at Your feet.
You alone can lift me up and
You alone make me complete.

In my body, soul and spirit,
I am hungry for Your touch.
Let Your presence overflow me.
I'm in need of You so much.

Lord, You suffered in Your body
and You bore my sin and shame.
Now I come to You for healing.
You can take away my pain.

You're my Anchor, You're my Fortress,
You're the Rock on which I stand.
You're my Comfort in the darkness.
You're the One Who holds my hand.

I will give You praise and glory
while in faith, O Lord, I wait.
You're my Everlasting Portion.
You are mighty, You are great!
--oOo—

(Psalm 121:1-2)

~~ QUIET MOMENTS ~~

Quiet moments, O Lord with You,
precious and so divine;
quiet moments, focused on You
are moments of peace sublime!
--oOo—

(Isaiah 30:15)

~~ BLESS FAMILIES ~~

Dear Lord, bless fathers and also mothers.
Bless all the sisters and also the brothers.

Grandmothers, grandfathers, uncles and aunts;
grandchildren growing as tender plants.

Lord, be the light that brightens their road.
Let peace and harmony be their abode.

When trials seek to tear them apart,
please send Your love to fill their heart.

Let hurts and wounds all be forgiven;
let love be the force by which they're driven.

May You forever be enthroned
in family lives and hearts and homes.
--oOo--

~ ~ EACH DAY ~ ~

Each day as I rise and open my eyes,
I see Your beauty in the skies.
As I look around, I must confess
Your awesome love, for I am blessed!

You brighten my path, my spirit You feed.
You always help in times of need.
You've blessed me Lord so very much.
Precious to me is Your wonderful touch!

Never could I have dreamt I'd see
this place, this hour, for You've brought me
through toilsome valleys, hills and plains;
You comfort my heart again and again.

Thank You that I can call You in prayer,
dear Lord – anytime and anywhere.
You're great and wonderful Lord, always.
To You belongs the highest praise!
--o0o--

~~ WHERE SHALL I GO? ~~

Where shall I go to find a friend
on whom I know I can always depend,
who'll hold me up and whose heart is warm,
who'll help me to stand in a time of storm?

When all I can see is a mist or haze,
when pressures increase and I'm feeling fazed,
when I need an anchor of hope for my soul,
when I need some courage to reach my goal?

When challenges come, I will run to You.
Though friends may fail, You always come through.
You're patient and kind. Your love is so pure.
When doubts assail, Your word is sure.

What a precious and wonderful Saviour You are.
You shine more brightly than any star.
How wonderful, Lord, is the peace you impart.
O Jesus, the joy of my heart!
--oOo--

(Psalm 73:25)

~~ I JUST NEED TO KNOW ~~

I just need to know it's You, Lord.
I just need to hear Your voice.
I just need You, Lord, to guide me,
then I know I will make the right choice.

Sometimes I have caused my own heartaches
when I've run on ahead with my plans,
only later to find You were waiting
there to guide me with Your loving hands.

O help me to listen always
to Your voice with my inner ear,
and to heed all the words You are speaking,
so my pathway will always be clear.

You promised, dear Saviour, to lead me
and to teach me the way to go.
Precious Lord, I am willing to follow,
when I know it is You, when I know.
--oOo--

(Psalm 32:8)

Chapter 4

Comfort in Sorrow

☙

"The Lord is nigh unto them that are of a broken heart, and saveth such as be of a contrite spirit" (Psalm 34:18)

~~ NOW THAT YOU'VE GONE ~~

Now that you've gone, what shall I do?
How shall I face each day without you?
Though you're at rest, in heaven above,
deep in my heart is a treasure of love.

Memories of you are warm and kind;
so precious a friend, it's hard to find
words to convey the pain in my heart
when deep within I am torn apart.

In moments of weakness, you were there
with a heart of love and a word of cheer.
You were a tower of strength to me.
You stood by my side and helped me to see

That faith in the Lord will help us to stand;
that He will guide with His loving hand.
Forever, I'll keep His promise in view,
the glorious hope that we'll meet anew;

When time will change to eternity long,
and together we'll sing a brand new song.
Till then, I'll cherish the treasure within.
So long, my friend, 'til we meet again.
--o0o--

(1 Corinthians 50:51)

~~ IT WILL BE WORTH IT ALL ~~

Roses in the garden of heaven,
stars in the glistening skies,
God's faithful ones now rest,
awaiting the heavenly prize.
The children of our Saviour,
perhaps to the world unknown,
perhaps on earth forgotten,
He'll call before His throne.

"Well done, good and faithful servants,
enter the joy of the Lord"
are the precious words that Christ will say
and they will receive their reward.
Though long the road they have travelled
and suffered and sacrificed,
it will be worth it all – one day
in heaven's paradise.
--o0o--

(Matthew 25:23)

~~ HE CARES FOR YOU ~~

If waves of sadness flood your soul,
take courage friend.
When nothing seems to help console,
it's not the end.

The One Who holds you up today
will be there tomorrow.
He'll make the darkness light and He
will lift your sorrow.

When you feel that the prayers you pray
are just a token.
The Lord will still be listening to
the words unspoken.

His everlasting love for you
will never wane.
He longs to mend your broken heart.
He knows your pain.

Though time has swiftly moved along,
there's hope anew.
The Lord will never let you go,
He cares for you.

When you are all alone, remember,
He is there.
Reach out and call His precious Name
for He is near:

*"O Jesus, precious Jesus – Lord,
I need You now.
O let Your waves of peace flow over
me somehow.
I come just as I am for I know
You are Love.
My help comes from You, Lord of earth
and heaven above.
O lift my soul that I may joy
in You again.
I'm trusting in You Lord, for You're
my greatest Friend"*
--o0o--

(Psalm 121:1-2; Psalm 139: 1-17; John 8:12)

~~ JUST A DREAM ~~

Precious the years of life together,
years that were only yesterday.
Loved ones gone, the days seem long;
now we are left to make our way.
A moment passed that brought us sorrow.
Now it seems hard to face tomorrow.
Deep in our hearts are memories of gold,
moments we cherish that never grow old.

Times of love and laughter together;
times of caring, whatever the weather;
times of joy and sometimes pain;
memories often return again.
In Christ, we hope one day to meet
our loved ones again, on golden streets.
On that great day, it will suddenly seem
those years of absence were just a dream.
--oOo--

(1 Corinthians 15:52; 1 Thessalonians 4:15)

~~ BLESSED ARE THEY ~~
THAT MOURN

The words of Jesus,
"Blessed are they that mourn".
His Spirit will bring newness
like the dawn.

He'll be your strength and
comfort deep within.
You'll rise again and mount
on eagles' wings.

Let Jesus be on board
your sailing ship,
He'll lift you up, although
you may have slipped.

Whatever the crisis
you may face today,
He'll hear your cry,
He will not turn away.

Though sorrow deep within
may cloud your view.
Know this, dear friend,
He truly cares for you.

For each and every pain
inside your soul,
His arms of love reach out
to make you whole.

His word of consolation
will begin
restoring you with healing,
fresh like spring.

His Spirit will bring newness
like the dawn.
There's hope in God for
"Blessed are they that mourn".
--o0o--

(Isaiah 40:31 and 61:3; Matthew 5:4)

~~ A DAY IS COMING ~~

A day is coming, take heart, dear friend;
a day when trouble at last shall end.
When Christ shall gather together His own,
to be with Him ever in heaven's sweet home.
When sorrowful tears He will wipe away,
when pain shall cease in that endless day.
When loved ones again will see one another;
fathers and mothers, sisters and brothers;
Aunts and uncles, daughters and sons,
grands and greats, everyone!
Where there will no more be clouds of the night;
where Christ, the heavenly Lamb, is the light.
Where joy and gladness forever will reign,
when Jesus, our Saviour, shall come back again.
Keep walking with Jesus and never give in.
Each day, He'll give you the grace to win.
That day is coming. Look up and be strong.
Hold on to the end, for it won't be long!
--oOo--

(1 Thessalonians 4:16-17; Revelation 21:4,23)

This poem of comfort was also published in Forever Grateful:

~~ BEYOND THE SUNSET ~~

The night was long and hope held on
for morning light to shine;
the darkness passed and paved the way,
but then arrived the time.
The Bright and Morning Star reached out
His tender hands of love,
a precious soul to welcome to
His heavenly home above.
The years of life seemed like a day
of memories to keep;
for now your loved one, tired and worn,
has entered into sleep.
Beyond the sunset, there is rest
and everlasting peace.
The light of glory ever shines
where life will never cease.
To all who place their faith in Christ,
God's promises stand sure.
One day we'll all be together again
in life forevermore.
Take courage now and as the future
in your life unfolds,
keep treasuring the memories,
for they are more than gold.

--o0o--

Special Prayer

Special Prayer:

Dear Friend ..
We have peace with God through our Lord Jesus Christ.
If you would like this, below is a simple prayer poem
which you may pray:

~~ COME INTO MY HEART ~~

I want to know You, Jesus.
I've heard so much about You.
I have some friends who've told me
You can make my life brand new.

I want to know You, Jesus.
They tell me of Your love;
that You came down from heaven and
that You're from God above.

I want to know You, Jesus.
They said that You forgive;
that You suffered and died upon a cross,
so that we might live.

Deep down inside my heart -
I want to understand.
I believe that You exist and
for my life You have a plan.

I've nothing much to offer;
in simple prayer, I come.
I do believe, dear Jesus,
that You are God's only Son.

I believe You died and rose again
to set us free from sin;
that all who come to You
can have eternal life within.

O come into my heart -
be my Saviour and Lord.
Please help me now to live my life
according to Your word.

I thank You, dearest Jesus,
for giving new life to me;
that one day I will live with You
in heaven eternally.
--o0o--

*(John 3:16; Romans 6:23; John 6:37;
Romans 5:1; Romans 10:8-9)*

~ ~ ~

*Thank you dear friends
so very much
for reading my poems.
I hope you were blessed
and encouraged
and pray that the Lord will
continually bring you
comfort and peace.
Amen*

~ ~ ~

ABOUT THE AUTHOR

Christine Mitchell enjoys writing heartfelt and uplifting poems of faith. She also writes poetry on other life topics and for special occasions. Christine came to faith in Christ in her teens and many of her poems are based on personal experiences on her journey with God. In youth and adulthood, she has faced some very difficult life challenges but has found love, peace and contentment within, through faith in God.

Christine has followed an administrative career and is also a carer. She has been blessed with musicianship skills and began writing songs more than 20 years ago. She has been married to her husband (and pastor) Frederick, for 34 years and together they have a wonderful family of 4 grown children (2 sons and 2 daughters), a lovely daughter-in-law and 2 amazing grandsons! Her first book of poetry, **Forever Grateful**, released January 2014, is filled with uplifting expressions of God's love, gratitude and encouragement. She gives God all the glory for this gift, knowing that He is the source of her inspiration. Her poems have brought reassurance, comfort and hope, and readers have shared how some poems brought tears. She looks forward to developing her writing skills further and also to writing her biography.

If you are going through difficult seasons in your journey of life, Christine invites you to explore this collection of her poems, where you will find words of comfort and consolation. If her poems have been a blessing, she would love to hear from you! She may be contacted in one of the following ways:

Via email: christinemitchellpoetry@gmail.com
her website: www.expressionspoetry.com
or blogsite: http://poetrybychristinemitchell.wordpress.com

Made in United States
North Haven, CT
05 February 2022